Dudley

DUDLEY

The Worst Dog in the World

AN ACCOUNT BY
COLIN WILLOCK

ILLUSTRATED BY
WILLIAM GARFIT

ANDRE DEUTSCH

First published 1977 by
André Deutsch Limited
105 Great Russell Street London WC1

Copyright © 1977 by Colin Willock
All rights reserved

Printed in Great Britain by
W & J Mackay Limited Chatham

ISBN 0 233 96926 8

This book is dedicated to anyone Dudley has ever fought, bit, terrified or enchanted. Also to those whom he has sometimes served and in his own way loves. It is dedicated especially to my wife, who nominally owns him, and to Julie who built a remarkable working partnership with him. Finally, it is for all Jack Russell owners who will know exactly what I am talking about

A Proper Little Boy

FAVOURITE dogs are usually best written about only after they are dead. That way, the good that they did lives after them. The bad is oft interred with their old bones.

This book is an exception. It is about Dudley. At the moment of writing, Dudley is very much alive and well, with every prospect of remaining so for some years yet, and living in deepest Surrey.

There may be some who will mourn this estimation of the unexpired portion of his life-span. I can only rejoice. To me, Dudley is a mini super-dog. When I say that he combines some of the qualities of Errol Flynn, Genghis Khan and the late Adolf Hitler – who, amongst other shortcomings of character, was said to fall down and bite the carpet when in a rage – you will correctly have guessed that Dudley is a Jack Russell terrier.

To begin at the nose, as it were, and continue on to the tail, Dudley was my daughter Jane's fault. With all the feminine wisdom of her then nineteen years, she had studied her mother's current state of mind, which I must say seemed pretty normal to me, and decided that now her children had pretty well flown the nest she was in danger of suffering from delayed broodiness. What she needed, diagnosed this junior psychiatrist, was something of her own to love and this despite the fact that she already had three grown-up young, a springer spaniel, an aged terrier, a cat, a horse and me. She was right about one thing. The remedy turned out to be Dudley and, as some have since said, only a mother could have loved *him*.

Dudley was born at Market Harborough. I never met his father or his mother. I understand they came from the most impeccable of Jack Russell stock, from the hunt kennels of two of the more distinguished shire packs. My contact with his lineage was confined to several engaging phone calls with a lady who described herself as a breeder of high-class Jack Russells, which some would claim to be a contradiction in terms. When questioned as to his character, or at least discernible indications of same at the age of six weeks, she described him as 'a proper little boy'. She did not understate the case.

Of course, one does not approach such transactions blindly. An experienced dog-owner knows all the pitfalls. So he puts his nose to the ground and sniffs the situation out carefully. Getting the wrong dog can be almost as disastrous as getting the wrong husband or wife. Moreover there are no easy rules for canine divorce. So, as a family, we approached the Dudley proposition with proper caution. That is to say we fell in love with his half-sisters. As a way of choosing a terrier this was probably more reliable than the method used by my wife in acquiring our previous Jack Russell. Not to put too fine a point on it, she saw him among a litter of puppies at a Christmas cocktail party. Full of Christmas spirit, or at least dry martini, she bought him, aged six weeks, on the spot. He was christened Toto, Swahili for anything small and young. I mention this because he had already been in residence some eleven years when Dudley made his first appearance. Toto played a significant part in Dudley's upbringing.

As a name Dudley has its African connections also. His actual given name is Dudu, the marvellously evocative Swahili word for insect. It seemed entirely appropriate. Insects are, after all, things that buzz around, get in the way, make nuisances of themselves and, incidentally, bite. So Dudu it was. Later, for reasons that partially escape me, it became

8

expanded to Dudley, though both names are responded to by the owner and are in common and equal usage. It was perhaps that Dudley seemed to suit particular moods of bantam cockiness, such as might be exhibited by a small, self-important and sometimes belligerent man of that name. There was something in the set of the tail that called to mind a pompously rolled umbrella.

I had better complete his passport with a picture that will be at least as accurate as the likeness usually attached to such documents.

Dudley is roughish coated or perhaps broken-coated. After reading all the books on Jack Russells, I am still not sure. One thing is certain: he does not resemble the good parson's immortal Trump but then few of the dogs today called after the founder of the line do so. He hasn't the long straight legs for a start. I would describe his front legs as short and Hepplewhite with perhaps a dash of Chippendale. The lower joints turn outward, rather like the feet of a Georgian silver salt cellar. His most sinister, and at the same time most appealing, feature is his face. Sinister because it is black, relieved only by two rows of teeth which a Nile crocodile would be proud to own. There is something Simian about that face, an illusion that is strengthened by the black, expressive, monkey-like eyes that show white only when the pupils are traversed, elevated or depressed to their fullest extent. Anyway, any adversary who leaves it until he sees the whites of Dudley's eyes is altogether too late. The jaw is somewhat crocodilian, too, none of your bird-beaked, little snouty jobs about Dudley. The black monkey face is relieved by brown eyebrows and by two brown cheek patches just forward of the ears. The latter, which seldom seem to be free of damage, are very superior models in terms of articulation and expression. On the fully alert dog they can adopt an arched, quizzical attitude which, depending on the degree of curve, can mean anything from 'Stop it or there'll be trouble' (half-arched) to (fully-curved) a polite and excited interest in any immediately useful

9

human's intentions. They also have a habit of standing bolt upright when the rest of the dog is lying down, dead asleep, or simply folding in half as if perfectly creased down the middle.

The rest of Dudley's white body is like that of a very thoroughbred vintage sports car, say a 1929 3-litre Red Label Bentley. That is to say it is packed for power rather than beauty but manages to achieve something of the latter by sheer, stark, functional economy of line. Like a good sports car it is long and low to the ground with just the right amount of clearance for cross country work. The power, too, is grouped in the back wheels. Grasp the muscles of a back leg and you get the feeling that if you ever had to eat Dudley to survive, which God forbid, a person could get a very fair, though toughish, meal off each of his rear drumsticks. Apart from two large black dots on his dorsal surface, one of which has spread since puppyhood to form a saddle at the nethermost end, there remains only the tail to be described. Like everything else about Dudley it is designed for use. Glory be, it was not docked. It stands upright when pleased in the manner of a running warthog's tail. When depressed, a fairly rare event, it hangs like a limp chipolata. Above all, it is an instrument for grasping. I have always believed that a hunt terrier's tail is left undocked for the sole purpose of hauling it out of fox and rabbit holes when that member is the only portion that remains visible and graspable above ground. I have certainly found Dudley's caudal appendage handy in this respect. He does not seem especially to resent the practice. If he does so, he has so far never succeeded in whipping his front end round sufficiently far and fast to make contact with his dental armament. I am, however, not relying on this always being the case. A friend of mine made the mistake of picking the same puff-adder up twice by the tail within a matter of seconds. The second time the snake had got things worked out. It drew first and bit him, with the result that he subsequently lost an index finger. Dudley is a fast learner, too.

I said that we bought Dudley, sight unseen, because of the appeal of his half-sisters. These two little girls, one whitish, one brownish, appeared regularly over several seasons in a friend's Land Rover at horse shows in which my guileful daughter was then competing. The two bitches were sweet, charming and tractable, altogether delightful and model Jane Russells. A postman would not have melted in their combined mouths. Gradually and cunningly, my wife and I were exposed to these miniature paragons. I give my daughter credit for brain-washing of KGB standards. Thus, when she finally revealed to her mother that what she needed was something doglike of her own to love, it was a foregone conclusion that we should approach the producer of the two diminutive girls, the breeder of high-class Jack Russells, for a similar model. How were we to know that the 'proper little boy' would turn out to be twice the size with an ego to match? How were we to know it would turn out to be Dudley?

Opening Bout

DUDLEY set the tone of his future life with us even before he had crossed the doorstep. He contrived to hold centre stage from the moment he left Market Harborough in a crate, courtesy of British Rail. There was a heatwave that day. There was also a dispute in some section of the BR Goods Department. For all I know it may have been about awarding danger money for operatives handling Jack Russells. If so, I have more sympathy with the cause of that strike than with most. My younger son, Simon, – Jane, the amateur psychiatrist's twin brother – was then a student in London. So he had agreed to take time off from his zoology studies to collect the new puppy. When two trains, including the scheduled one, had arrived from Market Harborough without the vital crate aboard, he began to activate things at Euston station, including the Station Master.

At a terminus of that sort, the Station Master ranks somewhere between an Admiral of the Fleet and a Four-Star General. In the ordinary run of things, the nearest he gets to a dog traveller, passenger or goods, is a short, meaningful stare at a royal corgi, warning it not to write 'By Appointment' on the red carpet.

It speaks well for the lad's activating abilities that he persuaded this dignitary that his railway had mislaid a valuable and costly animal and that something had better be done about it. It also speaks well for the Station Master, who moved with a speed possibly not seen on the northern region since 'Mallard' broke the world speed record for steam engines on scheduled services. Perhaps the Station Master himself was a dog-lover. Perhaps it was as well that he didn't ask just how valuable was the missing animal. The answer might have fallen short of his expectations: eight quid.

In less time than it takes to say 'Stevenson's Rocket', Dudley had been located in a siding north of Bedford. As a by-product of industrial action, his guards van had been dropped off and shunted. Since the atmosphere surrounding the dispute was taking its usual route, from bad to worse, there seemed every likelihood that the puppy would be stuck, without food or water, with temperatures rising hourly within his wheeled prison until he expired of asphyxiation or at least exhaustion. The Station Master, God bless him, wasn't going to have that. With all the authority that his gold braid commanded, he ordered his opposite number at Bedford to send a porter, hotfoot – in such temperatures it can hardly have been otherwise – up the line to obtain the captive's release.

My family has a gift for bringing bad news joyfully. All that morning, throughout the course of three different meetings, my office phone brought me bulletins regularly on the hour, and sometimes in between. By one o'clock, when we broke for lunch, my colleagues had a comprehensive, if one-sided, picture of the goods situation on the Northern Region.

For the sake of appearances I started by pretending that I was talking with some unknown freight agent about a consignment of missing film. This not unnaturally led to confusion at the other end.

'What the hell makes you think it's in a can?' Simon was loud, clear and understandably querulous.

'I agree the heat won't do it any good,' I said. 'Perhaps a porter will take it for a walk.'

'What is this?' the general manager said. He was a bit tired of the phone calls, too. 'A remake of Rin-Tin-Tin?'

At one o'clock Simon rang for the last time.

'I've got him.'

'How is he? Alive?'

'He is. I'm not. I'm going to have a large drink.'

'Well don't be too long. Your mother will be longing to see him.'

And that turned out to be the overstatement of the day.

I have a strange gift, too. It is for breaking in, all unaware, on a fraught situation with the conviction that everyone concerned has been having the time of their lives when what they've really been having might more correctly be described as the time of their deaths. I did it to perfection once on a wildfowling holiday with two old friends. Business had kept me from enjoying the first day's sport. I arrived at the pub for supper and burst into the bar with terrible bonhomie, shouting: 'Well, I suppose you've all had a wonderful day.'

At that moment one gun was lying upstairs with a bad attack of gastro-entiritis. The incandescently furious wife of the other was insisting he return home immediately. She'd apparently just heard that the boiler had burst. This lady was even then throwing his boots and cartridge bag out into the pub yard to add force to her argument.

And so to Dudley's own entrance.

It was a lovely summer's evening when I arrived home. Our garden is a place of peace and quiet, a glade in which to relax with a long drink after the stresses of a long day. In the train I had pictured the scene; my wife lovingly cradling the little child-substitute; my son, now recovered from the hot, desperate hours on Euston station, lolling on the sward drinking in, amongst other things, the tranquillity of the scene.

It wasn't quite like that. They were drinking all right. My son was also lolling, in a long chair whose resemblance to a stretcher was reinforced by the large bandage worn on his lower left arm. There was an unmistakeable bloodstain on his shirt sleeve. Both exhibited a glittering, we-were-just-waiting-for-you-to-turn-up flicker to their eyes that suggested they were both into, at least, their second large gin and tonic. In a panic-stricken flashback I saw those gumboots and cartridge bag describing a parabola through the night air of Norfolk. Even as the words were forming on my lips, I converted a happy: 'Well, how is he?' to a concerned: 'Well, how are *you*?'

My son held up a bandaged arm. My wife waved her glass in a rather woozy fashion. They were either slightly inebriated or in a state of deep shock: both, as it turned out.

The story came out fast.

Dudley arrived and was let out of his crate for introductions to be made, first to his proud owner – who I gathered swooned over him – and then to the two resident dogs, Teal, the springer spaniel, and Toto, the other Jack Russell.

Without so much as a welcoming sniff at the newcomer, these two immediately fell upon each other in bloody affray. The battle rolled through a herbaceous border and the musk roses until it ended up in the lily pond. The latter is more of a courtesy title than anything else, since what the pond actually contains is duckweed. Duckweed pond would be closer to the horticultural truth. There the contestants were gallantly joined by Simon, who, in trying to separate them, received a three-stitch bite on the forearm. My wife who broke a broom over the spaniel's backside, without noticeably influencing the issue, escaped with bruises. Eventually, possibly disgusted by a surfeit of duckweed, the antagonists released each other's ears, legs, jaws and throats, all of which parts had received perforations and lacerations during the duel.

Simon then retired to the local hospital for his tetanus shots and stitches, while my wife, still shaking from the experience, took the two survivors, more expensively, to the vet's for theirs.

To this day no one knows what precisely triggered the battle. In retrospect all are certain it was Dudley's fault or anyway Dudley's presence.

Dudley's reaction? It seems he sat there enthralled, as if

unexpectedly given a ringside seat for one of Mohammed Ali's greater fights. I imagine that he was delighted to discover that this was the kind of thing that went on at his new home. He may even have supposed that an exhibition bout had been arranged as a welcoming ceremony. And I have an uneasy feeling that the experience exerted a strong formative influence on his later years.

Worm-free

ALL puppies are captivating. Dudley was just more so. For the first week I was filled with anxiety that the jealous fury that Teal and Toto had turned on each other might now equally suddenly be turned on Dudu or, rather, Dudley. Though they bore the widespread and as yet unhealed scars of their recent battle, the two older dogs acted as though never a growl had passed between them. There was no guarantee that such peaceful co-existence would continue. If the puppy had, in some inexplicable way, been the cause of the explosion, might not the whole snarling, gnashing lot go up again, this time with the proper little boy in the middle? The proper little boy went his way as though neither the two dogs nor the family existed. He rumbled around the house like a miniature tank, barely bothering to change course for chairs, tables, other dogs or humans. He was constantly getting bowled over by obstacles moving or stationary. He showed as much sign of pain and distress at these collisions as a dodgem car. On one occasion Teal displayed some elderly spaniel irritation when the puppy tugged at his leg feathers and held him down with a paw placed in the middle of the back. Dudley's reaction to this was to growl so convincingly that the springer thought better of it and let him go. There were no more dog-eat-dog incidents over Dudley.

Dudley revealed some unusual and troubling character traits from the outset. At the age of ten weeks he appeared to resent strange objects. If a deck chair appeared unexpectedly in the middle of the lawn, he barked at it in the hope that it would make a false move. Only when he had made quite sure that it was not challenging his right to pass did he put his growl away. But, thereafter, for the next week or so, he would remind it of its place by growling at it each time he strolled by. The deck chair eventually learned its lesson and recognised Dudley's dominance. Only when it had done so was it tolerated, but by then Dudley was usually giving the treatment to some other threatening inanimate object, a clothes-drier or, in one case, a new barbecue stand my wife had rashly bought without asking Dudley's permission.

Even as a very small infant, Dudley had paws like a badger. He could sink a three foot shaft into a rose bed quicker than a fully-grown aardvark. Filling his excavations in was no use at all. He regarded this as a kindness. The soil was simply easier to loosen next time.

My wife, poor sweet soul, fussed about him in a manner

which made me think my daughter's diagnosis might have been right. She worried about him getting enough vitamins which was a bit like worrying about whether the Royal Arsenal had put enough TNT into a twelve-inch shell. She grew concerned about his teeth – a fear that was to haunt many people in different ways as his career developed. She ferried home a charnel house of bones to help him over his mythical teething troubles.

Among other skills, Dudley perfected an extraordinary canine ventriloquism. He could hang on to a bone while being lifted four feet clear of the ground, all the time producing a continuous rolling growl. He was prepared to keep this up longer than you could hold him aloft. I admit that I admired this feat greatly and used to show him off doing his airborne growl to visitors whose reaction varied from horror to sympathy. One or two who were owned by terriers themselves grudgingly acknowledged that it showed he was the right sort. The fact that I encouraged the little horror to show off like a precocious child should have been a warning to me. Even when I knew for certain that the captive audience's reaction would be a cold one, I persisted. Proud parents sometimes order their piano-pounding prodigies to play pieces with titles like 'Tranquil Moments' and 'The Old Mill' in order to delight defenceless strangers. Well, that, as I later realised, was just what I was doing. Dudley's moments, however, were far from tranquil and there was little doubt that the audience often felt that it was being put through the old mill. As my wife had already begun to say: 'You're besotted with that dog.' She was right. I was and still am.

I've forgotten at what age precisely we decided it was time to worm the puppy. I do recall that it was when Simon was awaiting his crucial first year BSc exam results. Our family gets hysterically keyed up about such things. When it comes to tension, apprehension and disaster, everyone is made to suffer equally. This at least demonstrates a certain neurotic solidarity. It is also very bad for the nerves.

One Sunday night we calculated that the exam results simply must arrive the following Monday morning. For once we were right.

At that time I had a phase of eating that strange mixture of nuts, raisins, oatmeal and, I suspect, chicken starter pellets, that had become popular among hippies, among others, because it was said to give instant boost and all the nourishment one needed in return for very little trouble in preparation. You just emptied some of this discouraging mixture into a bowl, and, if you wanted to make it even more exciting to the palate, added a little milk. It so happened that Dudley was also given a small bowl of the stuff for breakfast.

That Monday morning I blundered downstairs clotted with sleep to find an envelope with the inscription 'London University' branded in letters of fire on the flap. Here it was. Should I open it on behalf of the candidate? This might prove to be an intrusion on private grief. Should I take it upstairs and wake the young zoologist to learn his fate for himself? I couldn't imagine that he would be overcome with delight whichever way the results went. He likes his full portion of sleep. So I decided to let nature take its course. When I reached the kitchen my mind was obsessed with the contents of that envelope. I did, however, remember that I had left the puppy's bowl with two crushed worm pills in it on top of the fridge, alongside the cereal packet. I took a bowl out of the dresser for myself, poured in the mixture which, to my Monday morning eyes, looked like two of sand and one of cement. Then I filled Dudley's bowl. The boiling kettle made me wonder whether I could steam the envelope open and seal it up again before Simon appeared. While still pondering the ethics, or rather the practicality, of this proposal, I had begun abstractedly to eat.

It was just as I was finishing the last gritty spoonful that I happened to look down at my bowl. The letter D was written clearly on its side. A turn of a few degrees revealed the letter O. I didn't need to turn the bowl any further to know that a capital G would follow.

My first thought was: 'My God. I've eaten Dudley's breakfast. I'll need worming.' My second was, 'My God. I've just *been* wormed.'

Simon passed.

Dudley obviously didn't. At least, not that time.

As for me. I was worm-free for at least the next three months.

Daybreak on Dudley

WHEN Dudu – I feel I must call him by his given name from time to time – was three months old, we decided he was old enough to be taken to visit relatives – his half-sisters. My daughter was competing in a dressage competition. The two little Jane Russells who had been indirectly responsible for Dud's purchase would almost certainly be there.

Dudu had already had some experience of horses. My daughter, Jane, often took him to the stables with her where he enjoyed stalking imaginary rats in the straw and being bowled over by two resident collies. Horses were something he took in his stride. I believe he took them for a rather larger sort of dog, and, since he wasn't afraid of any dog, he certainly wasn't going to be put down by something on four legs that didn't even growl or bark.

At that time Jane had a large and very beautiful grey called Orwell Daybreak, known among the family as Orwell Bankbreak. Daybreak was intended to be an event horse but never turned out that way. Though he could jump a barn roof for fun, he didn't care to do so when the chips and the entry money were down. He did, however, a superb dressage test. If Daybreak had one other fault it was that he could sometimes be a pig to load. He was a pig that morning, advancing halfway up the ramp of the trailer and then skittering sideways at the vital moment. Eventually, of course, the beautiful idiot put a hoof over the edge of the ramp and, though the drop was only a few inches, became even more temperamental as a result. Dudu meantime was rushing about the yard, chasing and being joyfully bowled over by his collie friends.

We took Daybreak up again. This time he came stamping backwards down the ramp as if he meant to crash his hooves through the boards. His rearward impulsion took him well back into the yard. At that very moment, Dudu appeared at full bore. The puppy cannoned into Daybreak's off-hind and rolled over just as the other hoof smashed down. I felt the puppy's shriek of terror and pain right inside my stomach. The little fellow was lying on his back, whimpering, a red weal the shape of half a horse shoe already livid on his belly. I ran to the pup and snatched him up, surprised at the strength of my own feelings for him. His eyes were half closed but his body quivered. Jane and I carried him into the house where the kind lady who runs our stables wrapped him in a horse blanket and, when he began to stir a little, offered him some warm milk. The sloe-black eyes were alert and swivelling to catch the main chance as always. The nose wrinkled at the scent of the milk and the tongue snaked out to lap a couple of times.

We debated what to do. I suppose we should have taken him straight to the vet, and we both knew it. He seemed shocked, but in no special pain. There were no limbs broken despite the fact that one hind leg had been partly caught by Daybreak's clomping shoe. If he was damaged internally then there would be little anyone could do about it except give him a knockout shot. We were already late and the show was quite an important one. We laid him in the horse blanket on the front seat of the Land Rover. The horse shoe mark on his tummy stood out like a brand. It took us an hour to reach the show ground. All this time he lay on his back, eyes bright and open, making no sound but occasionally licking a hand held out to comfort and reassure him.

As soon as we stopped in the horse-lines, I lifted Dudu out and put him down carefully on the grass. I wanted to find out if everything still worked and dreaded the answer I might

23

get. The pup stood unsteadily for a few seconds, his back legs spread as if to help him balance. Or, was he standing that way because of some awful internal injury? The matter was resolved within seconds. A lady with two whippets on a tandem lead appeared round the front of the next box. Dudu uttered his famous growl, a little shaky in the bass notes perhaps, but still recognisable as a war cry.

Even as a very small puppy, Dudu never cared for dogs on leads and for some reason especially not whippets on leads. Possibly, with instinctive foreknowledge, he sensed them to be potential rivals in the rabbit coursing stakes in which he was to specialise so brilliantly later in life. Whatever the reason, he broke into a stumbling charge at the astonished whippets. Handicapped by the after effects of Daybreak's threequarter-ton hammer blow, he was, on that occasion, easy to catch. We apologised to the lady and explained the circumstances. Rather tartly, I thought, she wished him a full and speedy recovery.

We came second in the dressage but it was Dudu's day. We took him to the vet on the way home. The vet quite rightly, ticked us off for not bringing him in immediately. 'I'll give him a shot,' he said finally, 'but there's probably no need. I reckon if a train had hit him, the train would be lying on its side at this very moment.'

Mohammed Dudley's Diary

READERS may be wondering why I sub-titled this slim volume 'The Worst Dog in the World'. There are even members of my family who resent the slur. To me, Dudley is both the best and the worst. Strangely enough it is some of his worst qualities that add so strongly to his appeal. I can see that others may not share this view.

From the age of six months Dudley frequently demonstrated that he was an escapologist of great stature. Compared with him, Houdini couldn't have got out of a carrier bag tied with pink ribbon. Dudley was, and is, the Alfred Hinds of the dog business. Sink chicken wire into the ground to a depth that will discourage the most persistent fox and Dudley simply puts his paws into overdrive and disappears like a mole with a worm to catch. At first, we tried to confine Dudley to the garden with conventional barriers. As a pup, Dudley not only escaped himself but was chairman of the escape committee for others, often with disastrous results. He dug tunnels everywhere and, where the youthful Dudley led, the now sedate Toto followed. Two Jack Russells on the loose amid the bricks and mortar is a situation greatly disliked by postmen, milkmen and, in our case, our Italian gardener, Salvatore. To his credit, Dudley had a feeling for fellow prisoners. We had at that time two beautiful tawny owls, inevitably and coyly named Wit and Woo. The owls had lived quite contentedly in a large enclosure in the garden since they were reared by my elder son, Paul, as nestlings. They dined mainly on chicken heads, a few of which invariably fell to the floor of the cage. It is possible, of course, that Dudley just fancied a snack of chicken head. Those of us who are inclined to romanticise his exploits (not the writer in this case – I was fond of those owls) believe that Dudley aimed all along to give Wit and Woo their freedom. I know that in this instance, he wanted to get *in*, not out. He dug his tunnel, retrieved his chicken head and retired to the secrecy of a rhododendron bush to eat it. Meantime, the owls discovered that the base of their cage had been breached and, un-believably for owls, walked out. They were never seen again and though tawnies are frequently heard hooting round the garden, I fear the *ter-wit* is not from the throat of Wit nor is *ter-woo* the lovesong of Woo. Owls raised on chicken heads and dead day-old chicks do not usually have the necessary hunting skill to survive in the wild. So, number one crime on Dudley's record – owlslaughter.

Crime number two was even more reprehensible. It soon became clear that Dudley finds a fast moving target on the borders of what he considers to be his territory very hard to resist. I would have liked to have drawn a screen round the affair of the long distance runner. So, no doubt, poor chap, would he. He was one of those scarlet runners who appear like early Autumn migrants puffing through the streets at dawn or dusk. I always imagine that they are rugger players jogging off the summer's fat laid down in Ibiza or on the Costa Brava. They may equally well, for all I know, be goal-keepers or young executives worried about their cholesterol. It is all one to Dudley. All he needs is a glimpse of fast-moving white shorts. He got such a glimpse just as he emerged from a new and undiscovered escape tunnel he had mined beneath the wattle fencing. The jogger was at that very second passing his exit hole. With one leap Dudley grazed his left buttock, ripping his shorts as he passed. Having, so to speak, winged his quarry he brought him to bay against the front gate. The loneliness of this long distance runner was over.

We had now reached the stage where any canine argument conducted at that unmistakeable Jack Russell pitch was assumed to contain Dudley. So the frightened and now partially exposed runner was soon surrounded by members of the family seeking to call their dog off. The runner, surprisingly, did not demand a telephone to send for the police. Instead he seemed quite happy to break training. At least he came in and had a large Scotch with us. To show there was absolutely nothing personal in it, the dreaded Dudley sat on his lap and licked his face. It is typical of the dog's many facetted personality. He'd have had the seat out of other side of the runner's pants if he'd met him outside the house next day under similar circumstances. As it was we parted the best of friends. The victim even sold me two tickets for the police regional boxing finals. It turned out that this was what he was training for. Dudley had not only picked out an off-duty police constable but also a promising light heavyweight.

Next time out Dudley went a shade too far. It was the day

of my eldest brother's funeral. My brother was a great dog-lover and had, as a matter of fact, owned several fox terriers. He also once had a large airedale, the true rough and tough sort, none of your showy, boxy-jawed fops, called Boy. Boy fought everything in sight to a standstill, including a great Dane called Chaka, after the great Zulu leader. He damn near killed Chaka. Thus were Rorke's Drift and Isandlawana avenged in Church End, Finchley where we then lived fifty years after the last Zulu War. So I know my brother would have appreciated Dudley's commemorative gesture. It was just a pity that it had to be directed at a member of the family, my nephew Peter.

As in the case of the jogging policeman, Peter moved too fast. He was running behind schedule and burst into the kitchen unannounced to ask the way to the church. From an early age Dudley was always sensitive about the kitchen door. It was an area frequented by people he didn't much like, the gas and electricity men, the milkman and, of course, Salvatore, the Italian gardener. Had my nephew entered slowly there would have been time for recognition signals to be exhanged. As it was, Peter burst into the kitchen with all the easy grace of a tough American cop breaking down a suspect's door. His initial impetus carried him halfway across the kitchen. I am certain that all Dudley saw was a menacing blur of fast-moving brown. My nephew had on a rather trendy new brown suit for the occasion. Dudley did one of his Sam missile intercepts, nailing the lad rather more effectively than he had nailed the Bow Street runner – after all he'd had some practice since then – in the right buttock. The damage was rather more substantial this time. Besides a three inch rent in the seat of a new pair of pants there were actual toothmarks in the flesh to be added to Dudley's tally. In his defence I must say that he was immediately contrite once he had recognised his mistake. My nephew was very nice about it. As a family we are all more or less dog-lovers. My dear departed brother would certainly have been delighted with the episode, especially since my nephew arrived at the memorial service with the arse literally hanging out of his trousers. There'd been no time for him to change. Later in the day we fell to discussing with what inscription Dudley should be remembered when his time came. My wife favoured the simple classicism of 'Cave Canem!' It was one of my shooting sons who suggested the winning epitaph: 'Sadly Missed – with both barrels.'

When in the mood, Dudley bit all sorts of things. He once bit the leg of the television set, though I consider this to have been under extreme provocation.

It's often said that dogs don't connect the image on the cathode tube with events with which they are familiar in real life. This is the reason dogs don't bother to watch much TV, that, of course, and the fact that there isn't a great deal on the box deliberately beamed at a dog audience.

The first programme of which Dudley became a fan was 'Colditz'. A born escaper himself, it had its obvious attractions for him. But it was those Nazi guard-dogs he really couldn't stand. This and his murderous hatred of Salvatore suggested to me that Dudley is not keen to get into Europe, except possibly with his teeth. After the first appearance of the dastardly alsatians Dudley never missed an episode. Whenever they appeared, he hurled himself, barking, at the set. At first I was convinced that it was the noise of the German shepherds slavering on the trail of the latest escaper that rivetted him and that he wasn't aware of the picture at all. But then the BBC ran a knock-out competition for sheepdogs. Dudley didn't think much of the collies because they never came near to biting the sheep. To his way of thinking this would have been the obvious and simple way to herd them into the pen. Moreover, the sheepdogs, of course, worked dead silently so this time there was no sound track to draw and hold his attention. Just the same Dudley sat fascinated in front of the set, his eyes following the crouching and creeping collies' every move. Don't tell me dogs don't watch television. Dudley does, but then Dudley, for a dog, has a very high IQ – around 25.

The time he bit the leg of the set, he was, as I said, under extreme provocation. Clement Freud was on with Henry, flogging dog food. I'd like to believe that it was that peculiarly Freudian bloodhound that Dudley intended to savage. I have had reluctantly to discard this theory. The little chap continued to grind the leg of the television cabinet long after Henry had left the screen, leaving only the even more lugubrious features of the MP for the Isle of Ely in view. Whatever else he may be, Dudley could never be described as a Liberal.

When I started out to write this book, my wife, his proud though sometimes reluctant owner, suggested it would read like an extract from Mohammed Ali's diary of professional engagements. To make too much of the little fellow's talent for a punch-up was an obvious pitfall for his biographer.

However, it is no good blinking the fact that he is awfully good and rather free with what in boxing parlance used to be called his 'dooks'. I cannot overlook the one blemish on this otherwise faultless dogrose. Equally, it must not, for the sake of sheer sensationalism be over-stressed. My answer to this problem is to get it all over, or anyway the worst of it, in one chapter – this one.

There was the three-cornered fight over the cat, Genet, in which Teal, the springer, Toto, the old Jack Russell, and Dudley all shook each other. By that stage the cat had wisely slunk away, leaving the boys to sort it, and each other, out. There were no vet's bills after that one, just a good deal of blood on the kitchen floor. Ten minutes later they were all friends again.

The return match was fought at the same venue. The only difference was that, if the cat wasn't involved, I most certainly was. I was carving a turkey for a dinner party at the moment when war broke out. There are those who say that I am not at my best when carving a turkey, or carving anything else for that matter. It's true that I occasionally become obsessed by wild fears: that there won't be enough to go round; that I will end up together with the bird on the floor; but principally that it will all get cold before anyone has a chance to eat it. Naturally I manage to conceal all this beneath a steely calm. Why then, my wife repeatedly asks, do I find it necessary to shout at her for plates, to scream at the guests to for-god's-sake-sit-down, and generally to use foul language at a time when we're all supposed to be enjoying ourselves? One answer, of course, is that she exaggerates. I am renowned for my lack of temperament. Another is that, perversely womanlike, she insists on recalling and making capital of the time the carving got interrupted by a three-ring dog fight. It is not a moment I wish to recapture in its entirety.

What set the three idiots off I will never know for certain. It may simply have been the smell of hot, roast turkey. Dudley was certainly fielding in his customary position of first slip, slightly to the right of the carver's arm in order to catch any scraps that flew off the carving blade. Possibly he was encroaching on Toto who favours waiting for a catch at point.

My own belief is that the explosion was triggered by the growl and rasp of the electric carver – a loathsome instrument at the best of times. I was in the act of neatly dissecting a drum stick when I found myself with a whirl of snarling dogs about my legs. The guests were new neighbours whom we had been convulsing over drinks with some of our more repeatable dog experiences. It was my wife's clever way of letting them know what they were in for while they got a couple of swift snorts below the belt. Well, now they were finding out.

The dining room communicates with the kitchen by means of a service hatch, already opened in the reasonable expectation that large loads of steaming turkey were about to be shovelled through. What the hatch actually brought to the relaxed diners was a din apparently produced by a rioting pack of foxhounds, the sound of a broom handle making contact with unheeding dog flesh, a great deal of filthy language and the eventual thud of the turkey, as I had known it one day would, crashing to the floor.

We got that one sorted out, too, though it took two additional bottles of my best claret before the party settled to what you might call an even conversational flow. The new neighbours didn't stay long, as neighbours, I mean. The oil business moves its executives around a good deal. At least, I *assume* that's why they moved.

Then there was the riot in Cell Block 14. This was a straight contest between Dudley and Teal. Traditionally they shared a cubicle at the boarding kennels in which we always park the dogs when away from home. This establishment, run on exemplary lines by a former trainer of champion police dogs called Jim Duff, is irreverently known in the family as 'Duffy's Nick'. The two hardened criminals were

doing a month's porridge while my wife and I were away on a
film-making trip in Africa. Ever since Toto had sadly been
run over six months before, the springer and Dudley had
settled down to live together in perfect harmony. It seemed
as though all the previous strife had proved the old adage
that 'three is none'. Not so. The kennel maid never heard the
considerable din that must have accompanied the two old
lags smashing up their peter. When she went her rounds
half an hour after the last blow had been struck their cell
looked like an abattoir at the end of a busy day. The walls
were splattered with blood to a height of four feet. A quart
of red paint appeared to have been emptied all over the
springer. Only a feeble heaving of the flanks revealed that he
was still breathing. Dudley was red in tooth and claw, too,
but he was sitting up, panting, but obviously ready to go
back in there if necessary. The miscreants were called before
Governor Duff who sentenced them to an immediate visit
to the vet. I got the fine. A bill for thirteen quid for stitches
(in Teal) and anti-biotic (in both). The rest of their sentence
they served in solitary.

The Chain Gang

I HAD almost overlooked the affair of the intruding poodle. In winter it is comparatively easy to keep Dudley under house arrest except for regulation periods of exercise. The poodle, one of those clipped, snooty, miniature jobs, was on free range as Dudley had once been before he set out on his joint careers of escapologist and mugger. Throughout the whole of one winter the poodle made an insolent habit of visiting our garden and claiming every tree as a marker post to his territory. Dudley could sense him a mile off and when he finally appeared among the rose beds or on the lawn, the terrier dashed from window to window, threatening to chew his way through the glass and barking so that the plates rattled on the kitchen dresser. It was clear that if Dudley ever broke out when that poodle was around, the neighbourhood would be one dog short and it wouldn't be a Jack Russell. The poodle seemed to trade on the immunity Dudley's incarceration gave it. It poodled about the flower beds at an insolent dawdle, looking up at the murderous black face on the other side of the glass with the smug security of someone regarding a man-eating tiger from the right side of the bars. When the poodle piddled against a Scots fir which Dudley especially favoured, it did so, apparently, in slow motion. Beyond the window panes Dudley's teeth were gnashed and ground all winter long.

When the Spring came – his second season with us – it was obvious that we had a problem. Dudley must be permitted to enjoy the freedom of the garden with the rest of the family. On the other hand, neighbours, visitors, passing runners who might, or might not turn out to the off-duty policemen, must be allowed to enjoy their freedom, too. On Dudley's previous summer's record it seemed unlikely that he would permit them to do so. Pure genius – I won't say whose – came up with the answer – ten yards of lavatory chain.

Rope would have been useless. Dudley would soon have bitten through it. Lavatory chain was not only tooth-proof, it was sufficiently light to permit the little fellow considerable freedom of movement. With his chain anchored at one end to a tree, or even to a garden bench, and attached to a collar at the other, Dudley could indulge in most of his favourite sports such as fly-catching, bone-chewing, excavation even, and all this over quite a large area.

I went to see my friendly neighbourhood ironmonger.

Mr Waugh is one of the old school of ironmongers. He keeps mysterious articles in tiers of small odorous cardboard boxes. These contain things that people seldom ask for, and certainly never by the correct name, such as vine eyes and splitting wedges. Quite often, even though he knows exactly what you want, he allows you to continue to make long verbal descriptions and imperfect drawings of the article con-cerned, even to mime, while he stands apparently baffled and does nothing to help you. If he doesn't approve of you it is quite likely that he will send you away without a vine eye or splitting wedge, even though he has a vast unsold supply of these items. Some see this as cussedness on Mr Waugh's part and take their custom to a shop where the ironmonger doesn't even stock vine eyes. Personally, I view Mr Waugh's purist approach as a symptom of sheer professionalism and of proper pride in his trade. Sometimes, when he does agree to fetch down the required cardboard box, it still has the price pencilled on it in shillings and pence. Much of Mr Waugh's more esoteric stock has not granted official recognition to the decimal system. If he sticks to the price shown he is almost certainly selling at half the present value. Mr Waugh, however, is an ironmonger of his word. One of the many things he doesn't approve of is inflation.

Over the years, Mr Waugh and I have established a certain rapport. The relationship came near to snapping – and that, as it turned out, wasn't all – the morning I walked in and asked for ten yards of lavatory chain.

Mr Waugh is a tall man. He had a way of standing and staring like a stunned giraffe at customers who make ridiculous as well as inaccurately phrased requests. He is also exceedingly deliberate of speech.

'Ten . . . yards . . . Mr . . . Willock?'

'Ten yards, Mr Waugh'

A longish pause.

'That's . . . a . . . great . . . deal . . . of . . . lavatory . . . chain . . . Mr . . . Willock.'

You could see a mind attuned to years of weighing out meticulous ounces of one inch panel pins wrestling with the possibilities. Did my house contain ten loos? Could it be that for some mysterious reason I wanted to flush an upstairs loo from downstairs by remote control?

At last. 'Could . . . I . . . ask . . . what . . . you . . . want . . . it . . . for . . . Mr . . . Willock?' Mr Waugh does not like to see his wares misused.

'To tie up a Jack Russell terrier, Mr Waugh . . .'

Silence. Then: 'You'll . . want . . . brass . . . for . . . that.'

'Isn't that going to be rather expensive?'

'I've . . . only . . . got . . . brass.'

Now I know perfectly well that Mr Waugh has some cheaper chromium chain. I bought some for its proper purpose just a week previously. As a matter of fact it was this that gave me the idea.

'You'll . . . need . . . the . . . best . . . quality . . . for . . . the . . . job . . . you've . . . got . . . in . . . mind . . . Mr . . . Willock. Though . . . it seems to me . . . like . . . sending . . . a . . . boy . . . to . . . do . . . a . . . man's . . . work.'

This single sentence both left Mr Waugh master of his

craft as well as suggesting that only a lunatic would put good lavatory chain to such improper use.

The chain worked fine. All summer long Dudley pottered and pootered at the end of his tether without, if you see what I mean, actually reaching it – mentally that is. He seemed perfectly content with the restriction that enabled him to remain out of doors unsupervised. Provided you placed him in an area of lawn which gave him a full ten yards radius and movement through 360 degrees, with sufficient shade somewhere within the circle, you could leave him for hours on his own without the least danger of him getting tangled up. It certainly gave him more freedom than being shut up in a kennel and wire run. Often the anchor for his chain was a heavy cedar garden bench.

Dudley, in his second summer, was now developing the build of a miniature bull. His shoulders as well as his back legs were packed hard with muscle. If a wood pigeon or even a pied wagtail walked across the lawn beyond the ten yard limit, Dudley, true to form as always, reacted strongly. He sometimes built up such a head of steam over these intrusions that he charged with a force sufficient to move the heavy seat forward at least a yard. Once, when a Siamese cat did its business with fastidious mock-modesty amid the delphiniums, Dudley pulled the seat in a series of frenzied rushes halfway across the lawn.

All this time, Mr Waugh's best quality brass chain took the brunt. Gallantly it held out all summer, though one tended to forget that it was never forged for such savage work.

The poodle wisely stayed away all summer. It had got the word, no doubt, that there was something nasty at the bottom of my garden. This was good thinking on the poodle's part. Dudley, having become accustomed to the idea of being clamped to the landscape, was now quite frequently treated as a 'trusty'. Under supervision he was increasingly allowed free range, a privilege he seldom abused by wandering too far. Dogs are very much creatures of habit. He had come to accept that the immediate vicinity of the lawn was his exercise yard. Provided one kept both eyes on him, he did not wander off and break out over, or, in his case, under the wire. No number of eyes could have kept Dudley in vision, however, had that Siamese cat, or even worse, the poodle wandered in while he was chain-free.

When winter returned, so did the poodle. Along with the redwings who dropped in from Scandinavia to polish off the holly berries, the poodle was back from parts unknown. This was his nearly fatal mistake. One fine, late October day I decided to dig over part of the vegetable garden so that the coming frosts could get their teeth into the soil. Dudley looked at me beseechingly. At the time I thought he was just asking to be allowed a sniff round the garden. Thinking back on it I believe he had more desperate thoughts behind those eyes as black as the pit of his small dark soul. Those thoughts included break-out, murder or preferably both. Dudley could have starred in any canine version of a James Cagney prison movie.

So I let him come with me. For the moment the poodle was far away from my thoughts. It did occur to me, though, that Dudley could not be allowed free-range. The fall of leaf had thinned the hedge cover to the point at which the weaknesses in the fence system were open invitations to anyone of Dudley's talents. I moved the garden seat into the middle of the lawn and attached Dudley to the end of Mr Waugh's lavatory chain. He would be secure there while I got on with the digging.

Some back-breaking twenty-five minutes later, something snapped. It took me perhaps five seconds to realise that that something was Dudley's chain. By that time I was getting all kinds of audio feed-back which told me that we had a prison break that would have made the Warden of Alcatraz jump off his famous rock into the sea. The sounds included, in order: horrific growling of the sort Dudley makes when he is homing on the target and hasn't yet zeroed in on it; the swish and scatter of gravel being sprayed as if from beneath the spinning wheels of a car; finally, a crash of bodies hitting timber and the screams of a victim about to be done grievous bodily harm. I took in the scene as I ran, the furrows in the lawn made by the heavy seat as it shuddered forward to the first shock of Dudley's charge; the chain broken at a link cunningly weakened for just such a moment as this. Nothing under the size and power of a buffalo could have gouged those skid-marks in the loose gravel of the drive. On the far side of the road, Dudley had the poodle pinned against a white picket fence. By the throat. One upright of the fence had cracked under the impact. I picked the poodle up and shook him hard, hoping that Dudley would eventually drop off. I should have known better. At last I carried them both, still locked together, across the road and dropped them into the water butt. When Dudley still showed no signs of letting go, I held them under with a rake. The water started to go red, like a scene from 'Jaws'. After a time Dudley came up for air. I was ready for him and grabbed him by the neck, hurled him into the garage and slammed the door shut. When I returned, the poodle had made it back to the surface, clambered out and disappeared. He hasn't been back since.

Mr Waugh was right about one thing. It's no good sending a boy to do a man's work. I should have gone to a ship's chandler. Anchor chain with a twenty-ton breaking strain might just have done the job.

There Must be Some Good

EVEN the worst dog in the world must have a good side. Dudley has several. When not ripping up pants or poodles, he is an animal of melting charm. At least I find him so. I even, or perhaps especially, admire his independence. I have heard it argued that terriers are closer to the wolf-originated dogs – an aloof clan to which belong, among others, samoyeds, huskies, chows – than to the more gregarious and fawning descendants of the golden jackal who include practically everything else with four legs and a bark. Wolf dogs are by nature loners, attaching themselves, although tenuously, to one master or mistress at best. Dudley carries his detached nature, as he does everything else, including bones and slippers, to the furthest possible point. Dudley is a born mercenary, serving where the pickings are richest and fighting on only one side, his own. Since he belongs to my wife and spends most of his time in the same house with her, if not actually close by her, he seems to recognise that there is a bond of some sort. However his moments of overt affection for her, or to any other member of the household, are of the briefest. A quick lick, a condescending wag of the chipolata tail, a few seconds residence on a receptive lap (officially disallowed but in Dudley's case almost welcomed as a rare accolade) and that's your lot. In the evenings, individual members of the family may be favoured with such greetings, then he sneaks off to my study to lie upside down in the easy chair, head, also upside down, hanging over the side, nose towards the carpet. It is not a normal position for a dog but then Dudley is not a normal dog. Even though the heating is switched off in the study and the temperature there is decidedly chilly, he prefers this place and pose to lying stretched out with the other dogs before a roaring sitting room fire. The other dogs do not favour the study. Dudley quickly sized it up as a desirable vacant property suitable to an eccentric recluse and claimed it. He would far rather be cold on his own terms than warm on anyone else's.

Apart from the fact that he possesses unlimited charm, what else can be said in the little chap's defence? He is, it goes without saying, an excellent house dog, as can be judged from the fact that he even attacks relatives up to the rank of nephew when they have not given sufficient notice of their intention to enter. The fortunes I have shovelled away in terms of dog food over the years I tend to regard as burglary insurance premiums on a grand scale. When Dudley savaged the leg of the TV set, mistaking it for one of Clement

Freud's underpinnings, he was, in a sense, biting the hand that fed him. I certainly don't grudge Dudley his share of canned insurance premium. He would keep anyone from the door, possibly including the wolf. As evidence of the latter, he is allowing me to write this book about him.

In the early days of his reign of terror this paragon of a terrier demonstrated to no less a person than my mother-in-law that, as far as he was concerned, foxes are *persona non grata* around our homestead. Dudley would no doubt far rather have killed his first fox in a proper earth in decent hunting country. Failing that, Ashley Drive, Walton-on-Thames would have to do.

Foxes, as everyone nowadays seems to know, do very nicely among the dustbins and trim gardens of city suburbs. Nor are these the mangey critters some people would have you believe. This one most certainly was not. In mint condition it would have been a threequarter grown dog fox in excellent health and fine pelage. It was no longer in mint condition when Dudley, or rather his friend and occasional enemy the springer, Teal, delivered it muddy and bloody at my mother-in-law's feet as she was sitting down to cucumber sandwiches in the garden.

My wife and I were away that day visiting one of my sons. We had left my wife's mother in charge of the house and dogs. That was, as I now see, the basic mistake. Somehow Dudley had sneaked out and, calling for Teal on the way (I'm certain it was that way round), had disappeared in the direction of a neighbouring garden where workmen had some months ago demolished a large old family house and left the place derelict. Dudley's, or maybe Teal's, nose had told him that there was unfinished business to be conducted among the ruins. I can imagine the scene – the frantic digging beneath the piles of fallen brickwork. The fox surprised, all snarls and snapping jaws. Dudley darting in at the throat. The hand to hand fight among flying brick dust like some forgotten encounter during the siege of Stalingrad. Meantime, Teal, the second murderer, the mere accomplice, looks on amazed. When it is all over he perhaps feels ashamed in his soppy spaniel way that he hasn't contributed more to the heroics. Nevertheless, he is a retriever, isn't he? Well, he'd better retrieve something, if only his reputation. And so the pair arrive back, Teal carrying the slain fox as if it is a hare, Dudley trotting proudly by his side. Won't grandmother be pleased?

In fact grandmother shrieked and dropped the cucumber sandwiches. Later, being a lady of sterling qualities, she got a spade and buried the fox. After that she took Dudley upstairs and gave him a much needed bath.

Among his other mini-skills Dudley is a remarkable fly-catcher. He was not christened Dudu – insect – for nothing. Throughout the summer months he devotes a good deal of his leisure time to making life hazardous for anything with wings and six legs. He obviously has extremely proficient binocular vision, an essential range-finding requirement for most predators. As with a pike, or for that matter a crocodile, the long nose helps in providing a sighting plane. He spends many an hour when he might otherwise be biting postmen or other dogs, just hunting flies. He picks them up at maximum range, tracks them visually until they are within two or three feet and then leaps vertically in the air, often from a standing or even sitting start, crashing his jaws together with the sound of two billiard balls colliding at high speed. On warm summer evenings he turns to a night fighter rôle and intercepts moths in conditions of almost total darkness. Quite often I join in the game by providing illumination for him with a powerful torch. As with real night fighters during World War Two, searchlight cooperation often confuses the attacker. I fancy that he is more deadly and enjoys himself more when operating with unaided sight in conditions of bright moonlight.

Naturally, he does not kill every time. A high percentage of flies, especially, elude him, but he is never discouraged. As far as I can make out he does not particularly enjoy eating his victims, merely catching them. The spaniel, Teal, on the other hand likes eating flies. I have never quite managed to disbelieve the superstition put about during my youth by my mother that eating flies makes dogs thin. Though flies may not make them fat, they are undeniably of some protein value. Teal, who eats as many as he can get, is certainly overweight, though I doubt if flies are the only cause. Teal is too ponderous to catch them for himself. He usually makes do with Dudley's runners.

One encounter, especially, sticks in my mind. One summer evening Dudley had concentrated for several hours on a particularly smart bluebottle who had flown through his clashing jaws on at least six occasions. Finally, just as it was getting dusk, the bluebottle became a shade over overconfident and made a low level pass across the glass-panelled living room door. This gave Dudley a perfect crossing shot.

This time he was making no mistake and took off vertically. He hadn't, however, quite worked out the implications of the glass panel and though he hit the bluebottle literally slap on the nose – his nose – he also temporarily knocked himself out. While he lay there recovering, Teal walked past and ate the fly. End of scenario.

Good things to write about Dudley? He is charming to children and to properly introduced house guests. But then he is perfectly horrible to the postman, the milkman, the men who come to read the meters, the window cleaner and our much-loved Salvatore. I have tried over several years to acclimatise Dudley to Salvatore by taking him, on a strong lead, increasingly close to him. On the last occasion, after only three years of attempted indoctrination, mark you, I approached too closely and Dudley clamped his gnashers through the top of one of Salvatore's wellies.

Good things to say about Dudley? He is extraordinarily good in the bath. He stands there in warm water up to his hocks and allows a wet flannel to be placed over his eyes to prevent the soap getting in to them. It's a small point in his favour but, when you are scraping the barrel, anything you find in the bottom is worth putting on display.

At the outset, I feared that this might turn out to be a short chapter. It is, after all, about Dudley's good works and positive qualities. At the end of it all I can say is that he is certainly positive. I suppose that is why I am, as my wife, his owner, rightly says, potty about the little bastard.

Day at the Races

I wish I could claim that Dudley excels at the gentler terrier sports – racing for example. He's a little too stocky and solid to be really fast but he has a good stride and covers a lot of ground. It was this characteristic that prompted us to put him in for the Surrey Union terrier races.

Terrier races are the only track event in which the true climax occurs once the finishing line has been crossed. Since terriers are the contestants it follows that this climax invariably takes the form of a punchup. Terriers resemble football fans in that the game takes second place in their enjoyment to the chance of a good fight on the terraces.

Perhaps you have not witnessed one of these races. The course is about fifty yards long. At the starting end are miniature traps into which the little darlings are popped by their apprehensive owners. Just beyond the winning post stand the vital parts of an upside down bicycle frame. Instead of a tyre, the rear wheel carries a wire round its rim. This wire runs back in a continuous loop to a pulley fixed to the ground just in front of the starting traps. A fox brush – the equivalent of the electric hare in greyhound racing, though twice as provocative to these athletes – is attached. When the operator turns the pedals, the wire is wound in at high speed and, with it, the brush. Oh, one other refinement. In order to prevent the runners who finish the course from tearing the brush to pieces, the wire disappears under a length of sacking stretched tightly across the ground. So, of course, does the brush. Highly excited and deprived, as they see it, of their legimate prey, the runners usually fall upon and tear each other to bits just beyond the finishing tape. There the owners wait, hoping to scoop their entries up before serious damage is done. It is this final scene of chaos and strife that makes terrier racing the sport it is. It is also, I suspect the reason why most terriers agree to compete.

Dudley was well fancied in his heat. His opponents were three smooth-haired, short wheel-base models and a long-legged dog with a brown patch on one eye and a black one over the other. These patches gave the umpression that he was running in blinkers. That aside, he appeared slightly lame in his off-fore. He had been nobbled, possibly by another member of the fraternity, on the way to the starting gate. There were odd scuffles taking place wherever you looked.

As we came under starter's orders, I believe you could have got two to one on Dudley anywhere on the course. All went well until we were standing behind the traps ready to insert our runners. At that point, a mere spectator, a broken-coated dog who bore an unfortunate resemblance to Dudley himself, except that his muzzle was brown rather than black, was rash enough to growl something out of the side of his teeth. I don't know what he said but it was probably some reflection on Dudley's chances, more or less as though one race horse had said to another: 'You'd be better off pulling a milk cart.' Dudley's chances of winning evaporated at that precise moment. The odds must have gone out to fives, or even tens, as Dudley spun round on his lead and prepared to do battle. The other Jack Russell knew he was perfectly safe and continued to say things like: 'go chase your tail down an empty rat hole,' and other terrier pleasantries. From that instant, Dudley's concentration had gone. I slipped him into the trap. Narrow as it was inside, he somehow managed to turn round and face backwards to shout insults at his enemy who had, by then, mercifully been lead away into the crowd by his owner, or possibly trainer. Dudley was actually facing the right way when the lids of the traps flew upwards at the 'off'.

The fox brush held him to the business in hand for the first vital few yards. At the halfway mark he lead by considerably more than a nose. Then, alas, he caught sight of his adversary beyond the rails and, while still leading comfortably, peeled off sideways into the spectators to settle the only contest that really interested him. The blinkered dog, up to then a poor second, won the race, whereupon the three short-wheel base jobs set upon the victor. But the best scrap of the day took place half way up the course under a Land Rover.

To this day Dudley still considers that he won that race. But then Jack Russells have quite different sporting standards from the rest of us.

Dog Mafioso

APART from his unquestioned ability to keep visitors, both welcome and unwelcome, away from the house, Dudley, if he was to earn his keep, had to exhibit other talents. As a family we don't believe in keeping dogs that fail to work for their living. It was the unspoken hope of us all that the terrier, being of sporting ancestry, would prove an asset in the shooting field. At the moment of his signing on we were badly under strength in that department. Toto, the incumbent Jack Russell, was largely a recumbent Jack Russell. By now he was decidedly long in the tooth and had, over a long and honourable service, become bramble-shy. My old springer, Teal, had perhaps one more full season left in him. I could not possibly ask my wife to take on a fourth dog. We were, therefore, at low canine ebb. In these circumstances Dudley had to be thrown in to bridge the gap.

I have known shooting Jack Russells in my time. In Scotland I once shot with a pair of smooth-haired bitches who not only hunted but retrieved. More extraordinary still, the pheasants with which they came trotting back to their proud handler were all in one piece and more or less complete with feathers. Not a growl or a shake escaped these little paragons. This, as I immediately realised, was not likely to be Dudley's form.

I first took him to our Selsey shoot when he was barely five months old. To give him some hint of what it was all about we appointed an escort of two experienced terriers who might have been called his friends. At least he didn't fight with them.

Both were godfathers in the dog Mafia. One was his stable mate, the aged Toto; the other, one of the most charming of his race I have ever met. This was Harry, an adult dog whom Dudley grew up to resemble in size and shape if not in colour. Harry was brown where Dudley was black. This was by no means the only difference. If Harry was *always* Jekyll, Dudley, as the reader will have deduced, quite frequently transformed himself into Hyde. Harry possessed one of those almost too sunny temperaments. One meets them in people occasionally and wonders whether their owners are not just too good to be real. Harry, or Harold, (his surname was Wilson) at first sight seemed the ideal mentor to guide Dudley's first faltering pawmarks in the shooting field. And yet, was it so wise a choice? If Harry had a fault it was one deeply ingrained in the fraternity – a spirit of independence. Harry, so nice with people, could be perfectly beastly to rats, rabbits, voles and even field mice. The trouble was that he was dreadfully inclined, perhaps out of a sense of delicacy, though I doubt it, to go off and vent his beastliness on his own. I was relying on Toto to supply an element of steadiness.

Dudley's entrance on the shooting scene was not auspicious. He came out of the car propelled by the force of his own growl and attached himself by the teeth to the neck of an extremely forbearing yellow labrador called Nickel. Nickel not only did not know what had hit him, he could not see what had hit him. His dimunitive white assailant had made his attack in a blind spot just below the right ear. It must have been extremely irritating, painful even. Nickel just stood there wishing he would go away or at least let go. Dudley had no intention of doing either. Undoubtedly even Nickel's patience would eventually have become exhausted had not another member of the shoot, a man who invariably has everything for all occasions, remembered that he had a pair of gloves in the front of his Range Rover, designed to be worn when making barbed wire fences. Wearing these, and risking a fate far worse than anything mere barbed wire could have inflicted, this hero eventually unlocked Dudley's jaws.

Nickel, miraculously, appeared little damaged by the encounter and, even more miraculously, little put out by it. Subsequently the two dogs never spoke a cross growl to each other. The pattern was to be repeated with every dog on the shoot. One punch-up, and good friends thereafter. The thought has occurred to me that among the inner circle of Jack Russells this greeting ceremony to strangers may have some ritual significance, though I doubt if other dogs see it quite that way.

We then got on with the shooting, a simple day in September designed to stir up a few partridges, disturb one or two hares and generally to assert to the Sussex countryside that the shoot was back in business for another season.

As might have been foreseen, the two senior terriers were of little help as tutors. From the first step on the stubble they set off in separate directions about their own nefarious businesses. The farm at Selsey is intersected with brambly ditches, long, raised banks covered with blackthorn, and dykes, some of which eventually communicate with the sea, known in these parts as rifes. These banks and ditches make ideal settings in which an experienced terrier can annoy things for hours at a time in happy secrecy. From time to time, as the morning progressed, we would get news of one or other of them. Their actions were betrayed for the most part by their consequences, a bramble patch shaking as if caught in some tiny localised hurricane; a cock pheasant rising at two hundred yards range indignant because he had imagined he held a safe-conduct until at least October the first. On several occasions a rabbit made an exit closely pursued by Toto who had always been a bit of a specialist on the subject. For the most part Toto worked close, often within as little as one hundred yards of the guns. Harry was something else. Once launched, Harry was like a remote controlled torpedo whose electronic brain has become addled. In other words, though still filled with plenty of running, he was no longer controlled. He simply careered about on an unpredictable course, potentially lethal to whatever he touched. That morning he touched a great deal. At intervals Harry would appear from the depths of a ditch to pursue his relentless way across a field we were yet to walk, putting into undesired motion partridge coveys, hares, anything shootable that happened to lie in his path. He was not popular.

What of the infant Dudley all this while? Perhaps because he did not know any worse, he stayed more or less obediently to heel. Most the unwanted action initiated by his alleged tutors was fortunately too distant for him to imitate or to savour the future possible joys it promised. Like all puppies introduced to the field at too tender an age, he pottered about, bewildered. One would never take the risk of entering a gundog puppy at such an early age. Yet with Dudley I had the feeling that it didn't matter and would make no difference to his eventual value or performance. He had his one moment, however. Possibly remembering that he had once nearly received his come-uppance under the hooves of a horse, he challenged an entire herd of Friesian heifers to combat, prudently discovering that an electric fence gave him sanctuary, when needed, from their collective vengeance. Cattle worrying had to be discouraged and was so. Like many puppies, even Dudley did not relish being shaken by the loose skin under his throat, while master growled at him in a horrible voice. One lesson, at least, had been learned.

The last drive before lunch was through a small and often productive field of roots. I had been lucky enough to catch Harry as he emerged from a field drain at the conclusion of the preceding beat. As a precaution I had attached both him and Toto to lengths of binder twine. However, when all the guns were in position round the root field – I was a walking gun – I slipped the terriers believing that they would accompany myself and the beaters in a forward direction. Whatever they put up from this small field must surely fly towards one of the guns. I had overlooked the fact that the best rabbit bury on the shoot lay beneath a thick bramble hedge on the left hand side of the roots. Harry and Toto had not, however, and this time the puppy was close enough to them both to follow their bad example. Toto and Harry immediately turned left and made best speed towards the bury while myself and the beaters moved forward according to plan. It was only when we had flushed the one covey held by the roots and recovered the two birds slain that I realised all three terriers were missing. There was little doubt in my mind where they were. A rabbit bolted closely followed by Toto. I shot the rabbit off the end of his nose and caught him up as he pounced upon the corpse. One down and two to play, or rather one to play and two down. From the scurryings and thumpings it was clear that Harry was taking Dudley on a conducted tour of subterranean Sussex.

The rest of the shoot had arrived at a well-earned lunch break. Gundogs and their owners retired to a warm barn to enjoy a quick nip and a sandwich. The terrier man was not with them. Harry had gone to ground on strange territory, the puppy even more so. There could be no question of leaving them to surface on their own. Once above ground again they would have no idea where they were, let alone where to go. It had begun to rain and was miserably cold. I thought of the other guns sipping cherry brandy seated on nice warm straw bales in the barn. I thought, too, of Harry's bereaved owners. How could I break the news that I had lost their terrier for them? At home, the tidings concerning a missing Dudley might be more cordially received, though I doubted it. Just as the other guns emerged from the barn refreshed and ready for the afternoon's sport, Harry emerged fifty yards down the hedge plastered in red mud and ready for anything. A few seconds later Dudley appeared also. Dudley was covered in blood. I did not care to ask whose, though I devoutly hoped it was his own. After that all three terriers spent their afternoon in the back of the car. I imagine that they had had a satisfactory day since they were all asleep in a heap when we finally got back with nineteen and a half brace of partridges, a record for the shoot despite half a day's assistance by a posse of Jack Russells.

Entered to Game

DUDLEY came shooting fairly regularly after that. At first, I am convinced, he didn't in the least connect our activities with his own. He usually started the day by engaging in mortal combat with a new dog. These encounters were seldom harmful and more or less ritualised. The object, in Dudley's mind at least, was to establish that he was top dog. Once he had proved this to his own satisfaction with each dog in turn, there was seldom any more trouble. By the end of the first season he had worked through the list of resident labradors and springers and had only the occasional guest dog to sort out. Guests were usually warned to let their dogs off the lead if possible – Dudley cannot abide tethered dogs – and to dissuade their animals from making snide remarks at Dudley out of the sides of their mouths. The resident guns were remarkably tolerant of the little beast partly because they recognised him as a great dog character but also because he soon proved himself remarkably useful.

If this book ever earns its author a penny I shall be extremely surprised since everyone who has ever suffered under Dudley, especially my fellow guns, is guaranteed a free signed copy.

Dudley first showed his interest in shooting as a sport via ground game. The straw stacks on the farm were infested with rats. Brian, our part-time keeper, owned three dimunitive Manchester terriers who were deadly on rats, though they weren't much bigger than their quarry. One Sunday morning, on the principle no doubt of better the day, better the deed, the Manchester girls – they consisted of a mother and two daughters – polished off one hundred and twelve rats between them round the straw stack. There were a good many bales of straw in the barn where we ate our lunch, the same cosy barn to which I had been denied access by Harry's underground adventures. I seemed fated seldom to enjoy a peaceful lunch break on that shoot, for now Dudley, initiated by the three ladies from Manchester, had discovered the heady scent of rat. A midwinter picnic is not everyone's idea of social grace and gastronomic enjoyment perhaps. But a shooting lunch, warmed by a nip of sloe gin or cherry brandy, enlivened by the adventures and misadventures of the morning just past and given an edge by the prospects of the afternoon that lies ahead, is surely one of the most enjoyable and sociable of meals. Unless of course it is interrupted by scufflings, growlings and hideous squeakings, dashings and barkings and the seismic heavings of the very bales on which one sits. The cold game pie, or even the humble ham sandwich, cannot be enjoyed to the full when the diner is suddenly confronted at close range by a maniac face in which is imbedded a large and very dead rat. In the end Dudley's acts of murder, heard, seen and unseen, became too much for us all. All this coupled with the fact that when not ratting he tended to creep around drinking soup out of Thermos cups and stealing the odd sandwich, caused him, by unpopular demand, to be banished to the back of an open three ton truck which was parked in the barn. Surprisingly, he bore this sentence with resignation. Once he had established to his own satisfaction that even he could not bore his way through steel, he sat there and regarded us reproachfully through a small hole in the tail-board. He was, as I soon found out, merely saving his strength for the afternoon.

What he discovered one such afternoon – I forget which one but I know it was fairly early on in his career – was hares. That farm had hares like some dogs have fleas. They were always starting out of their forms in stubble and ley. They

56

streaked out from the tall grass alongside ditches. They
dashed suddenly out between the furrows of sticky plough
where there shouldn't have been cover for a beetle. Even the
steadiest of our springers and labradors were hard put to
resist them. Many a good and unwanted course was run, so it
was not surprising that Dudley quickly got the idea. The
dogs who did succeed in defying their masters never won.
The hare always got away with it. If a long-legged labrador

failed to catch his quarry, what chance did a short-wheel-
based terrier have? None at all, but in Dudley's estimation
this was no reason for not trying. He tried and tried. No
amount of harsh words and even harsher treatment dissuaded
him. To him, a hare was simply a rat on a grander and therefore more shakeable scale. Dudley's first actual tooth to fur
contact with a hare came very early in his initiation to the
shooting field. It must have occurred during his puppyhood,
in fact his first or second time out with the gun. It happened
during a partridge drive. I therefore know it was in the
September or early October of his first season. I remember
that I was one of the standing guns at the end of a long

stubble field, placed close to a gate. Hares have a marked inclination to make their exits out of fields via gates. A single covey came well towards the start of the drive. I took one out of it and so did the gun on my right. Dudley did not see either of the birds fall. His attention was rivetted on a brown shape bounding from the ditch on my left. The hare ran straight towards the gate. Dudley was gone before I realised it. I was vaguely aware of him in the right hand corner of my eye as I shot, tumbling the hare over so that dog and corpse met, head on. Dudley obviously regarded the hare's death charge as a personal assault. He seized the body by the scruff of the neck and shook it like a rat.

Picking the dead hare up by its hind legs, I did my best to shake Dudley free. He hung on in mid-air growling and shaking. For a good three minutes, I first shook and then cuffed Dudley. Holding some twenty odd pounds of hare and dog clear of the ground became extremely tiring work.

One of the guns walking the stubble towards us watched this drama take place from two hundred yards range. 'I couldn't understand what the white blob was. For one happy moment I thought you were trying to put Dudley in the bag,' he told me later.

As a matter of fact, I was. After several exhausting minutes I dropped Dudley, teeth still clenched to the hare, into a sack. Being suddenly plunged into darkness appeared to take the fun out of the situation for him. By the time the beaters reached us, Dudley had crawled out bloody and content that he had won a notable victory for which, he felt, we should all reward him. We did. He was shut in the car for the rest of the afternoon.

Dudley's natural progression had to be from fur to feather. Having discovered that he was not required, or expected, to wrestle with dead hares, he next turned his attention to game that fell, miraculously to his little mind, out of the sky. Falling pheasants were to him just another kind of rat, one covered with feathers. But whereas a hare will stand a fair amount of worrying by Jack Russell, a pheasant most demonstrably will not. It is liable to fly open, or even apart. Those horrible fangs leave marks in the succulent flesh of the breast that no amount of subsequent larding or covering with bacon

will cancel out in the cooking. At best, a pheasant given the once-over by Dudley looked untidy, possibly even unsightly. Moreover there was always the danger that a legitimate retriever might arrive on the scene at the same time as Dudley, or worse still just after he had gained possession. The advantage of such a clash of interests was that Dudley was quite likely to drop the pheasant; the disadvantage that he was more than likely to seize the other dog.

Stern, punitive measures were called for and, what's more, were ruthlessly applied. A hard shake by the throat and a fierce growl from master had far more effect on the puppy than any form of corporal punishment. He simply did not feel the latter and usually turned his attention to the stick or strap that belaboured him. Slowly he learned to abandon the worrying of slain fur and feather.

By the end of his first season he had become, if not exactly an asset, then not precisely a pest. In shooting terms he had still not done anything positive. On the other hand, he had ceased to act entirely negatively.

Dudley gets his Colours

BY the time next September came round he had ceased to fight the other guns' dogs. I believe this was because he now presumed that they all knew their place in relation to himself. It remained for Dudley to prove that he was of some use to the shoot other than as a persecutor and destroyer of rats. Though we were delighted to see the rat population discouraged – after all rats eat eggs, attack chicks and gobble expensive pheasant food – it was unlikely that Dudley would be awarded his colours for this service alone. He had too much to make up for. To be elected to the team, he would be expected to hunt.

Among his many talents, Dudley numbers remarkable, or at least unusual, eyesight. Not many dogs, for example, watch the telly. Attacking Clement Freud during his dog food commercials, or rolling on his back in ecstacy during those endless repeats of old Lassie films, argues a possession of some critical faculty rather than of exceptional visual acuity. After all, a dog does not have to be able to see more than five yards to watch the Box. But to be able to see *and* appreciate what he is seeing. That's quite a trick in itself. In the shooting field, Dudley was soon to prove that he could both see at great ranges and still appreciate what he was seeing.

I was walking gun at the end of a long strip of mustard on the day on which he demonstrated, early in his second season, that he dimly sensed that pheasants were what we ultimately required him to become excited about.

The mustard strip, planted as game cover, was every bit of three hundred yards long. We had surrounded it stealthily with standing guns. Teal, the old springer, Dudley and myself were waiting to go through with the beaters. Since he could do no damage if I slipped him – anything that was flushed out of the mustard patch must surely fly towards one of the strategically placed guns – I let him off the lead. For once, Dudley sat. Possible he was feeling tired. It was one of those occasions when I wished my companions could have seen the little chap, sitting like a field trial champion, gazing alertly ahead and awaiting the signal to move forward. A second later I was thankful no one was looking. A cock must have run forward out of the mustard as the guns moved into position. It now rose, unprompted by beater or dog, from a hedge thirty yards beyond the furthest gun. It took off a full fifty yards from the far edge of the mustard and was therefore at least three hundred and fifty yards from where Dudley sat.

The bird made no squawk of alarm to alert the terrier to its intentions. He saw it as it rose and rose himself, setting off at once to catch it, preferably in flight. His course and speed took him fifty yards into the mustard where, being enclosed in a dense yellow and green thicket, he became disoriented and forgot the original purpose of his mission. This can't have mattered too much to him since pheasants were now spraying out of the mustard in fair numbers to escape his progress. Whether we liked it or not, the drive had begun.

Dudley did not reappear until well after the beat was over. He had discovered so much simple pleasure in that mustard patch that he couldn't believe that pheasants would not continue rising from it as long as he cared to work it. To his credit he did put one cock out of that mustard that all the other dogs and beaters had somehow overlooked. A back gun who was late rejoining the main party shot the cock nicely and so Dudley, though not entirely popular with his handler, received for the first time some grudging praise for his efforts. When he at last emerged he had a new look in his black button eyes. He knew that annoying pheasants was thoroughly enjoyable.

One of the main features of the Selsey shoot were the long banks, possibly old sea walls but more likely born of the spoil originally thrown out of the deep rifes or dykes. The slopes of these banks were covered with coarse, tufty grass, ideal stuff in which a pheasant could shelter from the sea wind while gleaning weed seeds and an insect or two. At intervals the tops of these banks were clumped with impenetrable blackthorn bushes, impenetrable, that is, to any dog much over knee-high to a bank vole.

Having done the more formal set-pieces in the morning, we usually left the banks until the afternoon. There was no fool-proof way to shoot them. The two main banks ran parallel for almost a mile. The system was to dog them together, the beating parties moving in approximate synchronisation. Walking guns advanced with the beaters, between and alongside the banks, most of them ahead but some behind according to the wind, to catch the birds that broke back. Some storming birds were flushed and shot as a result of these tactics. It had to be admitted that a lot of pheasants ran forward into the blackthorn thickets from which they were seldom flushed.

After his foray in the mustard, Dudley was soon posted to the banks. This, if anywhere, was where he would prove his worth.

For the first couple of afternoons spent on the banks nothing much happened. The pup was once again in an unfamiliar element. He tended to scamper along at the heels of the questing labradors and spaniels, accepting their word for it that there was nothing worth looking for in tuft and tangle. Then, during his third term of duty on the banks, he blundered, probably by accident, into a cock pheasant that had cunningly sat tight and missed the attention of the other dogs. Dudley pushed his small nose into a thick tussock of rank grass, probably in pursuit of a field mouse, and out rocketted a positive jabberwock of a cock pheasant which curved away on the sea wind to soundly beat three back guns, one after the other, rising spectacularly as each salvo whistled astern

63

of its tail. Dudley, of course, got the credit for his initiative. I saw to that. At that time, Dudley was so short on good deeds that I was glad of anything that, so to speak, put his account in the black with the other guns.

The accidental flushing of that cock was, in fact, a turning point in Dudley's working life. The rampage in the mustard had been fun and, though pheasants pushed over the guns had been its by-product, it had to be admitted that Dudley had been acting blind in there. To him that mustard must have looked as tall as elephant grass. Smell and sound of pheasant he almost certainly got. Sight of same, he did not. Now as a result of his intrusion into the grass clump on top of the bank, scent, sound and sight of a bird urged into panicky flight by his own enquiries were all three locked on in his tiny computer. In one glorious eruptive second he knew what this was that we all came here for. The facts of shooting life were suddenly his. Most important to the little fellow, whereas most of his other favourite pursuits were frowned upon, or even violently discouraged, pheasant flushing appeared to be something master as well as otherwise unreasonable friends welcomed and even applauded.

He had no more luck that particular afternoon. Naturally there were those – chiefly the guns whose dogs he had at some time fought – who maintained his success was a one-off, a blinding doggy fluke. Sooner or later, they said, he would have been bound to have stumbled on something. The argument was a reasonable one. After all Dudley did cover a lot of ground in the course of a day spent in pursuit of his own highly individual business. I knew better and said so. I was the only one who had actually been there, seen the ears cock, the nose wrinkle, the stance stiffen into what was virtually a mini point. Then the determined dart into the secret place that had hidden the cock from all but the sagacious terrier. Wild chance, the scoffers insisted. Dudley had probably winded a beetle. He was known to have a great partiality to a juicy stag-beetle. I didn't argue.

64

A fortnight later the doubters were, as I knew they eventually would be, discomfitted.

We were on the banks again. Dud and I were working behind a long-ranging black labrador called Gus and even further behind another ditto called Trigger. Both labs were apt to get carried forward by their own enthusiasms. Give them a sniff of a running pheasant and they were off. In fact, it was often said of Gus that while we shot in Sussex, he shot in Hampshire and occasionally Surrey, depending on the direction in which we were taking the drive. The only way to deal with this deplorable situation was to have walking guns far enough ahead. There were several occasions when 'far enough' turned out to be not nearly far enough. With their single-minded attachment to one captivating scent, it followed that these two free-lances frequently over-ran birds that were sitting cunningly tight. Even if Dudley had had the legs to keep up, which mercifully he hadn't, he wouldn't have had the nose for such a headlong chase. He therefore pottered along well in the rear of their flying, and frequently cursed at, heels. Until the affair of the cock flushed from the grass, such pottering had been more or less aimless. Now, however, it was most assuredly aimed.

On this historic afternoon, Trigger and Gus had gone far, far ahead in pursuit of a bird that must have been anointed with all the perfumes of ancient Colchis, China and Mongolia from which its ancestors sprang. When the bird itself sprang, it was far beyond the reach of the most forward walking gun. Gus and Trigger began to retrace their steps with a false contriteness that suggested that the chase had been well worth any punishment in store. The pursuit had taken them several hundred yards past the blackthorn thicket into which their headlong hunt must, by all previous experience, have driven several pheasants. On their return journey they reached the blackthorn bushes half a minute ahead of Dudley and, having arrived at that crucial point, sat down to await what was coming to them. They knew the thick and prickly blackthorns of old. They were no place for a smooth-coated, long-legged labrador. Master they were prepared to face, but not a barbed wire entanglement into the bargain. This was an error of judgement on their part. Had they decided courageously to burrow in amongst the spikes, their reputation and hides might yet have been saved. In their defence it must be said that they were upwind of the thicket while Dudley was downwind. All the olfactory signals were therefore blowing in his direction.

At the vital moment I was just behind him, urging him on from time to time with a gentle gumbooted shove in the rear end. Something in his attitude told me that there would be no need to shove him into the blackthorns. Six feet short of them he paused and raised one front leg like a midget pointer. His nose twitched and the black button at the tip swivelled from side to side. He advanced cautiously over the open ground, as if expecting another cock to leap from the grass in front of him. Obviously the signals were reaching him hotter and stronger. As he neared the blackthorn patch his pace increased until he had sufficient impulsion to plunge under the portcullis of spikes. For half a minute nothing reached the outside world except the sounds of scurryings and snappings of twigs. Unlike some terriers, Dudley never gives tongue, not even on rabbits.

The first cock pheasant came through the roof of the thicket like a ball leaving the toe of an international full-back. He was flying all the way up, thorns or no thorns. Once in clear air, he curled away back on the sea wind to be shot, as he headed for the coast of France, by the last of the back guns. Two hens followed. They left by the front door, whipping over the heads of the sitting Gus and Trigger and climbed steeply. Both fell to flank guns well out in the plough. At that, the two labradors rose in a hurry and began to sniff at the exit hole used by those hens. They would have been too late to join the action even had they been prepared to get down on their knees and wriggle into the thicket. Dudley was now chasing around beneath the bushes like a mad rat. In the centre, the thicket was fairly open. The trick was to reach the scene of operations and he alone had successfully performed that. The chasing and scurrying was caused by the fact that the birds could run around likewise. When Dudley got too close to the tail of one of them, it simply sought sanctuary in the outside wall of thorns which was all of three feet thick. After his initial successes, the terrier had to flush each pheasant individually. It was rather like winkling well dug-in defenders out of deep bunkers.

The line of walking guns had halted and rightly so. In the next three minutes Dudley flushed six more pheasants out of that small patch of blackthorn. As I remember all flew well and all but one were shot. When Dudley emerged he was green from the mossy deposit that grew on the ceiling of the dark, dank cave in which he had been operating. But he was covered in something else, besides – Glory. I held him up so that all should know whose feat it had been. That day he was awarded his colours. He became an official member of the canine search-and-destroy team though, as one gun said, one could only hope that the accent would continue to be on search.

Guess What Dudley's Getting for Christmas

CHRISTMAS, 1975, coincided with Dudley's first shooting season. His full potential had, therefore, been revealed, in several ways.

The above headline appeared in the national press as part of an advertisement for Parker Pens.

The Dudley referred to in the advert, as a picture confirmed, was, of course, Dudley Moore.

Some member of the family cut the headline out and stuck it on the notice board in the kitchen, adding a hand-written note that suggestions would be welcome for the *real* Dudley's Christmas present list.

Practically all visitors come and go in our house via the kitchen. Over the pre-Christmas period a number of suggestions were added by those who knew and loved him. They included:

1. A visit to a dog food factory, preferably inside a tin.
2. A year's stay at 'Duffy's Nick'. (Jim Duff runs the strict and efficient Pressberg boarding kennels.)
3. A new lead – with all-mains attachment.
4. An exploding Irish stew (it was the time of the bomb outrages).
5. A box of crystalised postman.
6. A Jane Russell.
7. Gold, frankincense and GRYRRRRH!
8. A day's shooting with a good firing squad.

Dudley's Game Book

As rough shoots go, Selsey was an excellent property. Its great attraction lay in its variety. I suspect that Dudley found this factor alluring, too. Until I persuaded him otherwise, Selsey provided him with such a wide variety of fur and feathered 'rats' to shake. On any single day the bag could include, besides twenty or thirty pheasants and a partridge or two: mallard, teal, snipe, golden plover, redshank, curlew, wood pigeon, stock dove, hare and rabbit. Alas, as good shoots go, it finally went. The farmer wished to sell. Obviously the farm, which had no farmhouse, would be more attractive to a buyer if the shooting rights went with it. At short notice, eight friends, some of whom had shot together for eighteen or twenty years, found themselves without a shoot.

From all points of view the position looked hopeless. All of us could have found individual guns – at a price. Two or three might even have managed to transfer to new ground together. But the attraction of shooting lies largely in the enjoyment of the company of those you shoot with. I am tempted to add 'including your friends' dogs', but not everyone may wish to join in that sentiment. Biassed I may be, but I like to think that now that he had proved his worth, no one would wish to be separated from the talents of Dudley. Of course, I may be wrong.

So we did all the obvious things. We advertised and we put the word around. We got lots of replies to our advertisements but none of the shoots offered within easy range seemed quite right and those few that seemed perfect – and lay within our means – were all too far away. In the end it was word of mouth that did it. It usually is. One of the guns' children was at school with the children of a charming chap who ran some very high-powered shooting on a big estate near the South coast. It so happened that the estate no longer shot 1,000 acres of mature woodland bordered on one side by 300 acres of farmland and was looking for a keen and knowledge-able group of guns who would resucitate it as a shoot. It had formerly been shot by the big house and in its time had produced some notably high-flying pheasants and a great many woodcock. Moreover the estate was willing to rear birds for us and supply the services of a young trainee keeper.

It didn't take an extraordinary annual general meeting to persuade all concerned that they were being offered a one in a thousand chance. Naturally my first thought was: what would Dudley think of it? I fancied I knew the answer.

In fact, it was ideal terrier country. Beneath the mature oaks, chestnuts and beeches the ground cover was just thick enough to hold and interest birds and to prevent them from running ahead. On the other hand, keen labradors and spaniels might tend to cover the ground too fast. I saw Dudley's function, correctly, as a mopper-up of pockets of resistance left behind by the longer-legged workers. My daughter-in-law, Julie, had emerged during the last season as an excellent beater and dog-handler. She could even handle Dud and appeared to get great delight from doing so. He certainly responded to her and the team came into its own at the new shoot in a big way, the woods ringing to a bell-like voice crying 'get in there Duds' and just once or twice 'come here you little bastard'. In Julie's hands, Dudley responded, more or less, to kindness.

That first season he persuaded to become airborne a great many pheasants that would otherwise have been missed. Those that subsequently weren't missed are recorded in the game book. I have often wondered whether Dudley truly regarded the shooting of pheasants as the real objective of the day. Certainly not as far as he was concerned.

If Dudley could have kept a shooting diary for that season I am sure the entries would have been distinctly 'various'. Below I attempt to itemise some of the highlights that he might have featured in its pages.

Rowland's Castle Shoot, 1976.

Oct 30.   Opening day. No new dogs so merely gave the old ones a growl to ensure all present knew their place. Surprised a hare in a bramble patch. Far easier to chase than over open ground at Selsey. Think I will enjoy this place. Cornered young cock pheasant against rearing pen. Didn't know Julie used words like that.

Nov 14.   Keeper produced very nondescript terrier. It must belong to distant Hampshire branch of the Russell family. Born wrong side of the kennel, I shouldn't wonder. At right moment will have to teach it to mind its language. Pheasants getting up everywhere. Rather boring. Nearly missed second drive. Down rabbit bury at time.

Nov 28.   Black labrador called Tinker – stupid name for a gundog – growled at me at start of last morning drive. Been asking for it all day so I gave it to him in the left ear. (He won't need that one pierced if he ever decides to wear earrings.) Old labrador friend called Nickel – peaceful type since I clobbered him first time we met at Selsey – joined in and bit wretched Tinker where the squirrel keeps its nuts. Result Tinker shifts grip and gets my head in his mouth. Quite happy there since I have firm hold on scissors of his jaws. Stalemate. Fight unfortunately stopped by referees. It took four of them. Guns seem to have had a good day, too.

Dec 7.   Best outing this season. Caught cock by tail feathers and killed rabbit among blackberries.

Dec 20. Finally settled it with Tinker. Couldn't stand him whining at a rabbit that I had marked down for myself. Bowled him over and shook him by the throat in middle of third drive. Don't anticipate any further trouble there.
(*Note* Dudley was wrong. Master caught most of the *flak*.)

Jan 7. Earned good marks unexpectedly. Found and retrieved woodcock apparently shot two drives previously and given up as lost. Would have eaten, or at least given the bird a good shaking, but it smelt quite revolting. No wonder other dogs passed it by. Even Tinker's owner deeply impressed by my effort. Idiot!
Thoroughly enjoyed first season. Hear they are introducing two new guns with so-called good dogs next year. We'll see about that. Still, it's something to look forward to during the close season.

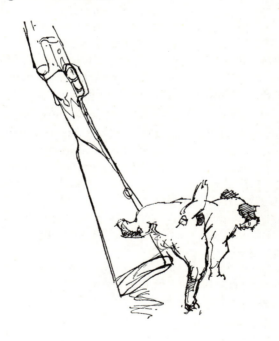

Dudley's Good Deed

ON Christmas Eve, 1976, the postman tipped twenty-five assorted envelopes through the letter box.

Twenty-four of them enclosed Christmas cards.

The twenty-fifth contained a bill for several hundred pounds, being the final payment of rental on the woodland shoot which we all enjoy so much, Dudley included.

By some uncanny trick of nose – perhaps the sender had been dispensing pheasants as Christmas boxes just before the bill was posted – Dudley smelt it out. And ate it.

The only decipherable words on what remained were: 'Amount due . . .' It was no longer possible to tell *what* amount.

I phoned the estate secretary after Christmas and explained. At the magic words 'Jack Russell', she said sweetly: 'It sounds very possible. I'll send you another one.'

It didn't come for a fortnight.

Expenses of the Christmas season being what they are, none of us was exactly disappointed at having two weeks' grace.

So there is some good in Dudley after all.

Tiger Essence

By now you will probably have reached the conclusion that Jack Russells are unmanageable, even untrainable. This may well be true, though I stress that I am accounting for only one of his race. Even though he is often called The Worst Dog in the World, Dudley has his tractable moments, especially when spoken to in a sufficiently gruff voice. Much as I love him, I wouldn't claim that Dudu, Dudley, Dud, Duds, the Dude, to list but a few of his pseudonyms, is easily cowed. And, sooner or later, in every Jack Russell owner's life comes the undoubted need to cow.

An actual cow isn't any good. Dudley demonstrated this early on in his career when routing that herd of Friesian heifers. There is, however, one animal that produces the required reaction. This is the single proven fact of inestimably valuable new knowledge that I am able to pass on to all once and future owners of Jack Russell terriers.

The animal concerned is not always easy to obtain. I refer of course to the Bengal Tiger.

How do I know this? One night we had a tiger to stay with us. It wasn't a very large tiger. Tara, a female cub, was about four feet long from nose to tail. She arrived at our house in the company of the well-known Indian conservationist, Billy Arjan Singh. In his native land, Billy specialises in rehabilitating big cats, that is in returning them to the wild. His farm at Dudwa, on the borders of India and Nepal, called Tiger Haven, has become the nucleus of a new National Park. At Tiger Haven he had already successfully reintroduced a hand-reared leopardess to the jungle. The leopardess unexpectedly called Harriet, subsequently mated with a wild leopard and produced two cubs which she brought back to the safety of Bill's house when her jungle den was threatened by monsoon floodwaters. Now Billy was about to repeat this feat with a tigress – Tara.

Tara was born at Twycross Zoo. There is no difficulty in persuading tigers to breed in captivity but there is considerable difficulty in persuading them to breed in the Indian jungle, largely because there is not much true jungle left. Tiger country is fast being replaced by the villages and farms needed by a constantly growing over-population. Tigers need a lot of territory in which to hunt and live. They eat domestic animals, occasionally people, and, I strongly suspect, dogs, including Jack Russells. Such places as Tiger Haven and the new National Park at Dudwa are about their last hope in India. Some of these areas are deficient in tigers. Hence the plan to restock by returning young females like Tara to the wild.

Tara came to stay the night with us because we were friendly with Billy and because we live within twelve miles of London Airport whence the little tigress was due to leave for India in the early hours of the following morning. We had an empty loose-box in the garden, an ideal overnight miniature tiger haven.

Billy had already spent a week at Twycross with Tara, just sitting in her enclosure, talking to her softly, getting to know her in fact. It was too much to expect that she would want to know anyone else, especially as she had spent all day travelling down the M1 from Warwickshire in a large crate.

My wife had visions of playing with the cub in the garden, possibly she saw her as a playmate for Dudley. I even indulged this fantasy myself. Tiger and terrier, regardless of difference in size, seemed a fair match. Whatever he felt about dogs, Dudley got on rather well with cats, or, anyway, with our own tabby cat, Genet. As it emerged, we were both very far in our imaginings from reality.

75

Tara was carried down to the loose-box in her crate. She emerged shyly and revealed herself as a meltingly beautiful young lady but certainly nobody's plaything. She had already become firmly attached to Billy, sometimes by her meat-hook claws, as the scratches on his arms revealed. In two or three days we might all have got to know each other sufficiently well for her to gambol freely on the lawn, perhaps even with Dudley. After the long day's journey by van and with the prospect of an even longer next day's journey by air, Tara was in no mood to greet and be nice to strangers. So we admired from the stable door, stroking her gingerly whenever Billy, and Tara, allowed. She was one of the most beautiful animals I have ever seen, the more so because we felt we partly owned a real tiger if only for one night. We were slightly carried away, too, by the thought that here we were, entertaining a tiger in outer suburbia.

The dogs? Under the circumstances the dogs had to be kept shut up. And yet, with that extraordinary prescience dogs often exhibit, they knew that something very unusual and rather upsetting was going on. When Billy came into the house they greeted him in an unusually subdued manner. Dud's chipolata tail hung limply between his legs. Teal crept away into his basket as soon as he decently could. Billy smelt of tiger!

We boxed Tara and loaded her into my Land Rover by torchlight at 4.30 am the next morning. Had the neighbours chanced to look out of their windows, I cannot imagine what they would have thought we were doing: certainly not what we were actually doing. Body-snatching, just possibly. Tiger-loading, most definitely not. Dudley, securely shut away, did not know either. All he knew was that we were up to no good as far as he was concerned. He barked throughout the entire operation, even though I twice went in to pat and reassure him.

The cockney loaders at Pan Am's cargo section took the tigress far more easily in mid-stride than had Dudley. We got a chorus or two of 'Tiger Rag'. The foreman ostentatiously put down a saucer of milk. Another loader trailed a length of rope up the vast, empty hanger, calling out, 'come on tiger, nice tiger, follow me tiger'. But they had seen it all before, or, if not actually a tiger, then something very like it. They had loaded lion cubs, a week or two previously. To them Tara was a pleasant break from the small hours routine of loading crates containing gear-boxes and lubricating oil.

Billy Arjan Singh and his orphan disappeared into the air travel limbo with the foreman's reassurance that they would meet again when the Jumbo stopped to refuel at Teheran. I returned rather sadly home for breakfast.

Dudley did not bound to meet me as he usually did. Even my faithful old Teal remained sullen in his basket. All the spirit seemed temporarily to have gone out of the dogs, especially the dreaded terrier. He crept around the house as if expecting to be pounced upon by something with which even he was unprepared to compete.

When I got back from office that evening, I took Dudley down to the loose-box on a lead. Just before he reached the stable door his brakes locked solid. Nothing would persuade him to proceed a single paw-mark further and it would have been cruelty, even to Dudley, to have forced him.

Dudley normally regards the loose-box as a convenience built expressedly for his convenience. On cold, wet winter evenings this has its points. Straw is easily and hygienically changed and his habit keeps the garden tidy. His routine — Teal's also, not that he ever used the stable for a similar purpose — was now completely upset and it was the tigress that had done it.

Dudley had heard of cats but whatever it was that had passed by, just beyond his horizon, was in his opinion carrying the whole cat business to ludicrous extremes. Neither dog can ever have encountered anything like a big cat in his life, and it is hard to imagine that the canine race has even a vestigial memory of giant prehistoric predators. Nevertheless they were both terrified out of their lives by the smell of tiger.

It was a full week before Dudley would venture anywhere near his favourite comfort station. When he at last plucked up courage to do so, he ventured in a foot at a time and, when a mouse rustled in the straw — at any other time he would have been on it in a flash — he shot backwards out of the door as if he had touched an electric fence with the tip of an exceptionally wet nose.

After ten days he began to enter the stable with great reluctance. Having plucked up courage thus far, he either forgot what he had come for or else was put completely off his stroke by the lingering aroma of tiger. For some weeks after Tara had begun her new life at Tiger Haven, he tiptoed around the straw as if in a minefield, pausing to sit up like an otter in order to sample the infected air at a higher level.

Tara is the only thing I have ever known to put Dudley down.

So my genuine and original offering to fellow Jack Russell owners is this. If you are having trouble in asserting your

78

dominance, run, do not walk, to your nearest zoo and obtain a bottle of genuine, one hundred percent, tiger essence. Uncork it whenever the situation appears to be getting out of hand.

Tailpiece

WHAT is there left to say about Dudley? A great deal, I fear. At the moment of writing he is barely four years old. Judging by the life-span of some terriers I have known, another ten, full, rich years may lie ahead of him. He still has a lot of living to do and, as has been demonstrated, he tends to cram a lot into the time available.

How can I sum up the multi-facetted personality of the creature that some people have called 'The Worst Dog in the World'? Perhaps best by adding my own considered and unbiased opinion of the little horror.

As far as I am concerned Dudley is, and probably always will be . . .

THE BEST DOG IN THE WORLD.